TIM JEFFS ART
Animal Sketches
REPTILES
past & present

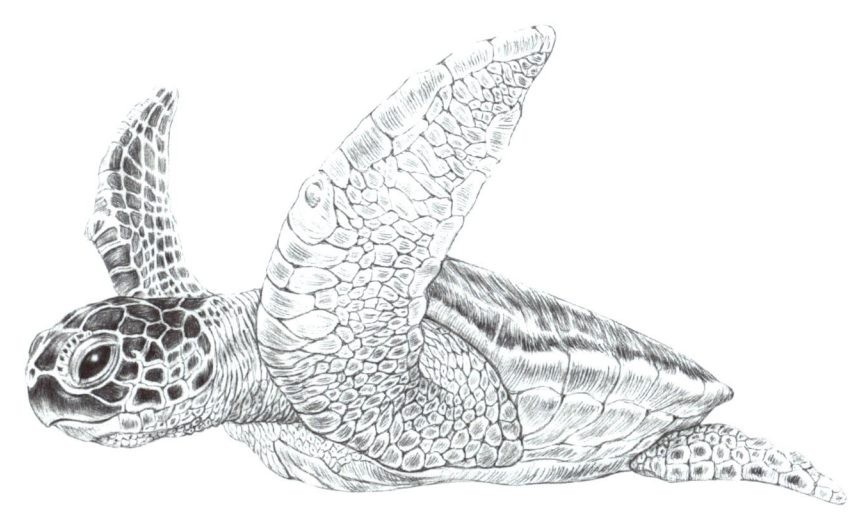

A Special Edition Coloring Book

For Jane, Jenna and Harrison

Dedicated to all of the wonderful colorists who have supported my art and made my drawings more beautiful with their colors, and all the precious creatures that we live among.
A special thank you to Jo Warren for all of her continued support and beautiful colorings.

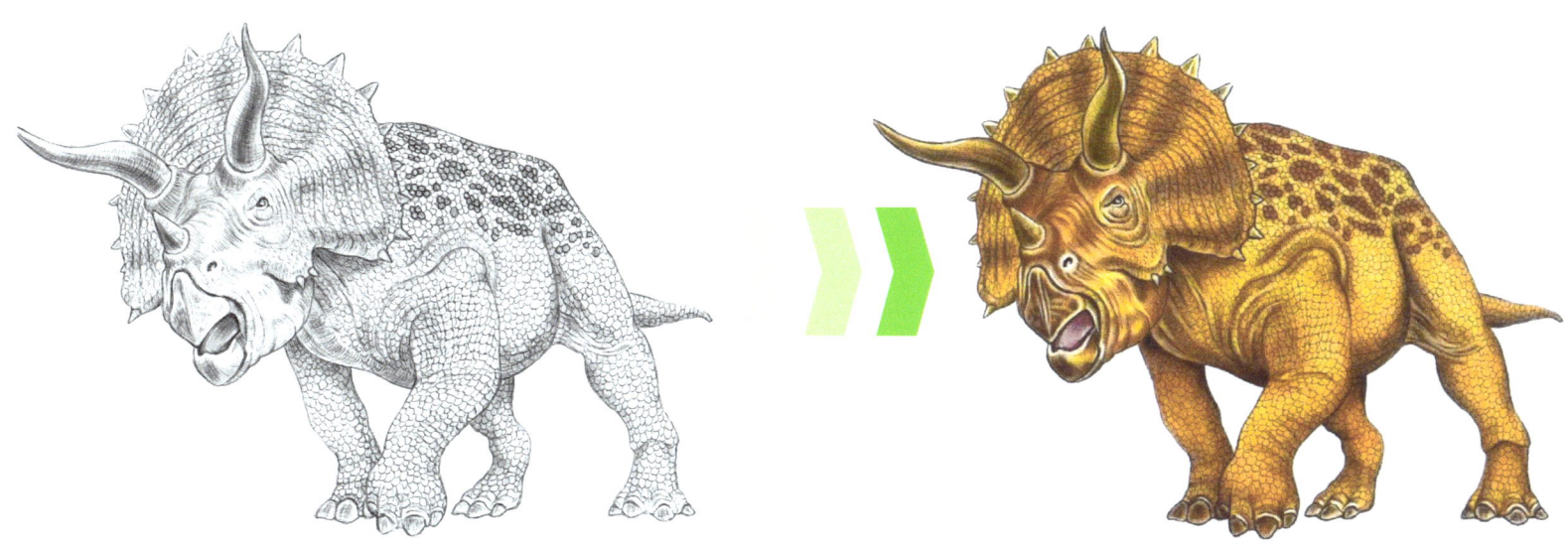

© Copyright 2021 Tim Jeffs Art
All rights reserved. No part of this publication may be reproduced or distributed in any form without the prior written permission of Tim Jeffs Art.

Tim Jeffs Art
376 East Madison Avenue, Dumont, NJ 07628

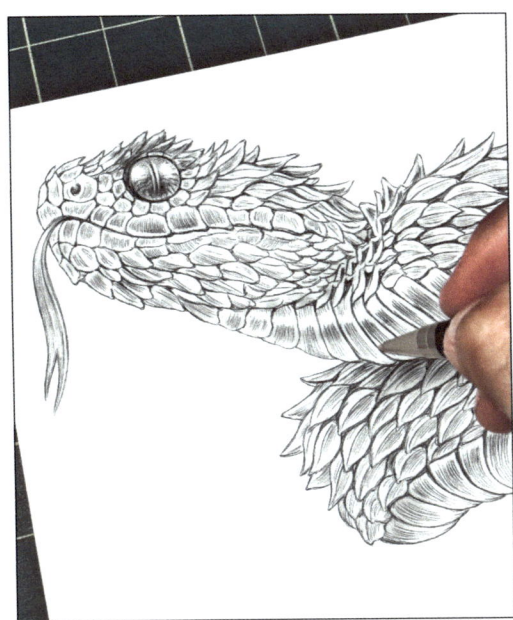 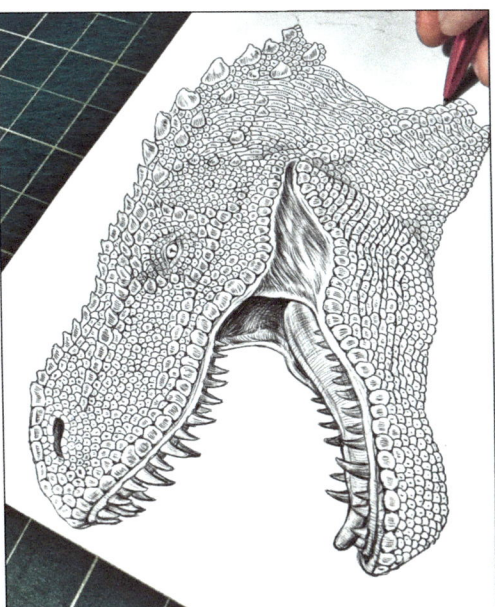 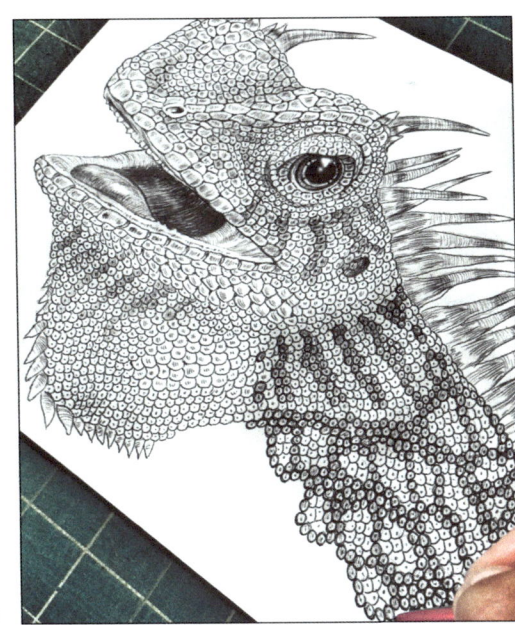

Reptile Sketchbook Thoughts

My artwork typically features portraits of animals who still inhabit the earth. As I selected the creatures I wanted to include in this Special Focus edition on reptiles, it occurred to me "how could I create a coloring book about reptiles without including a few drawings of the greatest reptiles that ever walked on planet earth?"

Dinosaurs, or as the word means "fearfully great lizards," need to be a part of this collection!

These incredible extinct reptiles have fascinated me since I was a child. I'll never forget the first time I visited the National History museum in Washington DC. As I walked into the Hall of Dinosaurs, my jaw dropped opened in awe as I stared at the skeleton of the Tyrannosaurus Rex towering above me.

I spent hours sketching skeletons, then my imagination ran wild, as I added details to these creatures who ruled our planet for so many millions of years. I hope you enjoy coloring this group of reptile sketches as much as I enjoyed drawing them, and I know that with your colors, you will bring them to life! Have fun!

GRAYSCALE COLORING LESSON
Tyrannosaurus Rex

lesson level: **Intermediate**

Coloring the
TYRANNOSAURUS REX

On the next page I will walk you through the coloring of the Tyrannosaurus Rex which is on page 15 of this coloring book. I have always been fascinated by dinosaurs. In 1841 the paleontologist Sir Richard Owen formally named dinosaurs, which means "fearfully great lizard". Rex means "king" making Tyrannosaurus Rex the "King of the lizards". This beautiful coloring of the T-Rex was done by Jo Warren. Many thanks for her creative and inspirational step-by-step photos.

❯ Supply List

In this lesson, Faber-Castell Polychromos Colored Pencil were used, (pencil numbers listed below) but you can use any brand with similar colors.

1) The coloring page can be found on page 15

2) Colors: Raw Umber #180, Grass Green #166, Kotel Sanguine #188, Olive Green Yellowish #175, Warm Gray #270, Black #199, and a Uniball Signo Broad Tip White Gel Pen was used on the white highlights

3) Pencil Sharpener: An electric pencils sharpener is easy to use and works best to keep your pencils extra sharp and your hand less sore. But if you don't have one, no problem. A hand pencil sharpener works just fine too.

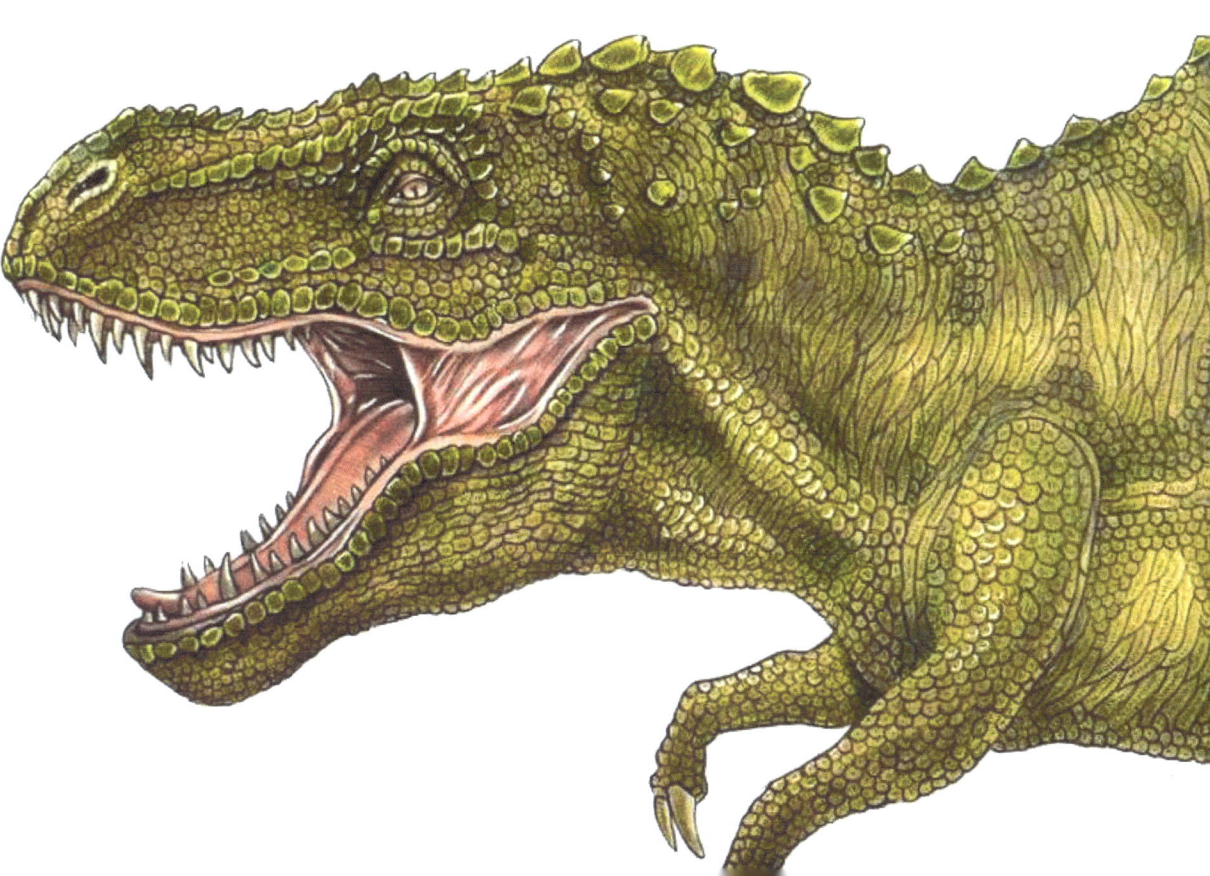

GRAYSCALE COLORING LESSON
Tyrannosaurus Rex

TYRANNOSAURUS REX
Supplies needed: 6 colored pencils and a white gel pen.

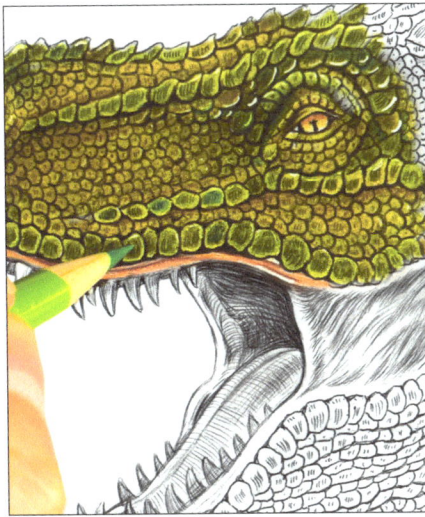

Step 1. Start by coloring in the scales on the T-Rex with a base layer of (#180) Raw Umber. To add depth add layer (#166) along the edges.

Step 2. Next, accent the larger scales with (#166) Grass Green. This will make the larger scales appear to project out.

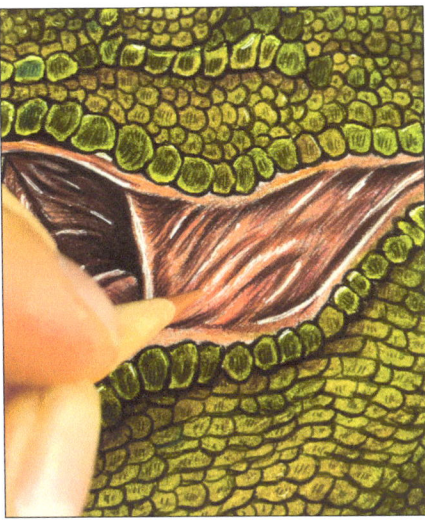

Step 3. To color the inside of the T-Rex's mouth first use (#188) Kotel Sanguinel, leaving the edges and ridges white so they pop out. Next use (#199) Black to create depth.

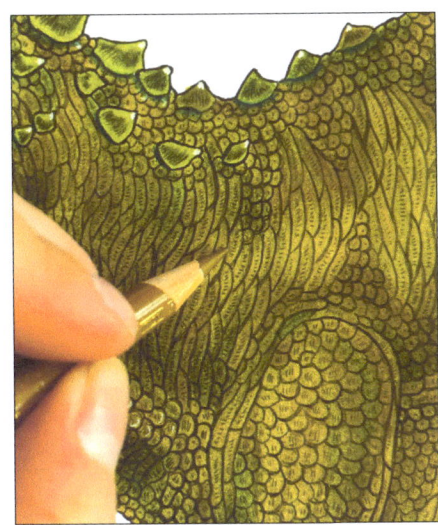

Step 4. Add a layer of (#175) Olive Green over your base layer of (#180) Raw Umber in areas to create shape to your T-Rex.

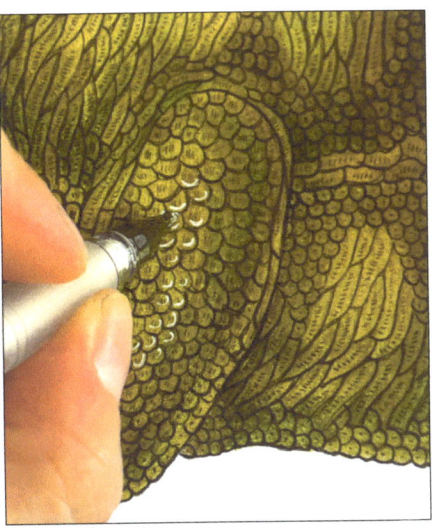

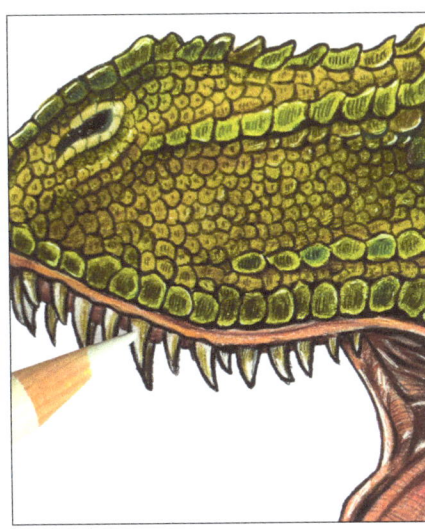

Step 5. Highlight some of the scales toward the center of the arm, around the nose, on the tip of the thorns and on the neck with a white gel pen.

Step 6. Color in the teeth with (#270) Warm Gray and then put a small highlight in the center with your white gel pen. Last, don't forget to give you T-Rex a unique colored eye.

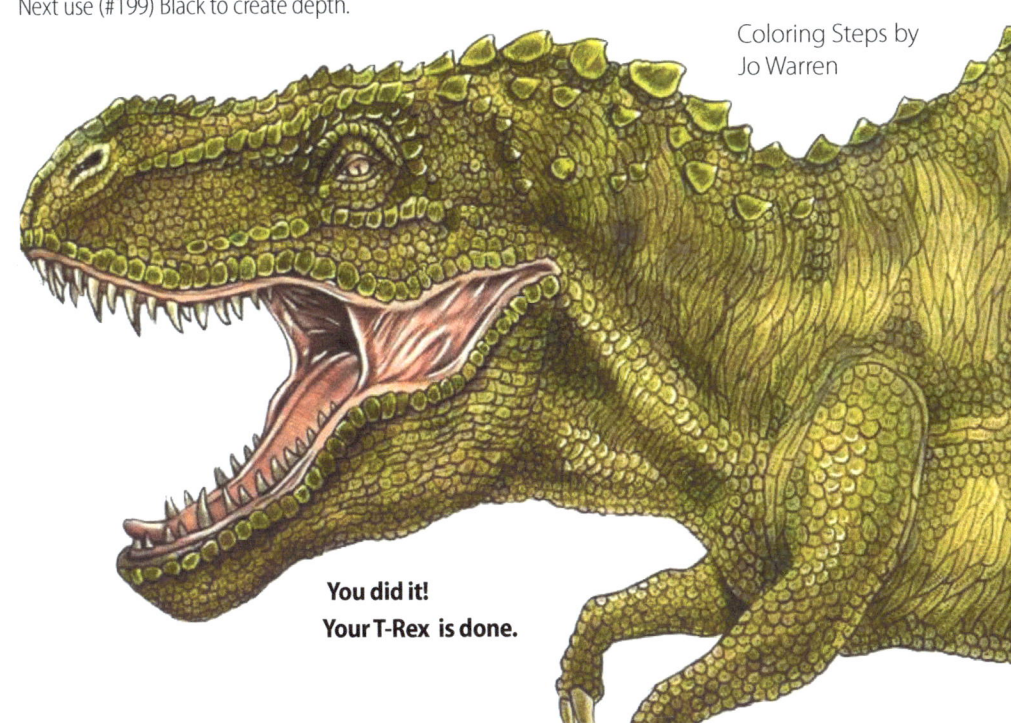

Coloring Steps by Jo Warren

You did it!
Your T-Rex is done.

Spreading Awareness through COLORING

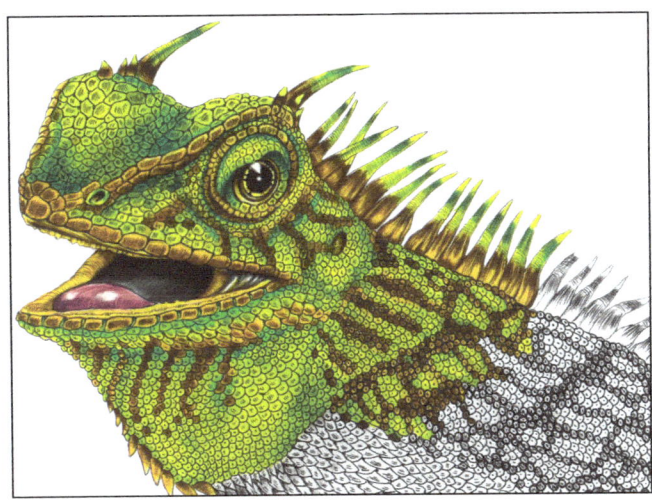

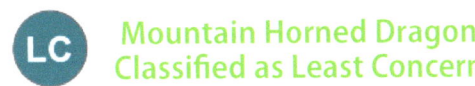
**Mountain Horned Dragon
Classified as Least Concern**

I truly believe that raising awareness through the sharing of my artwork is a fantastic way to educate people about conservation. And coloring animals is a beautiful way to learn about them as you enjoy a relaxing and fun pastime. On the following page, I listed reptiles' statuses on the *International Union for Conservation of Nature's (IUCN)* conservation list. I think it's important to include the *(IUCN)* conservation list so people understand the classifications more clearly. To the right is an overview of the IUCN's conservation list, which breaks animals' conservation statuses into several categories. Knowing what these categories mean and the animals that are included in them is extremely important. **Together through art we can change the world!**

Tim Jeffs
Animal Artist

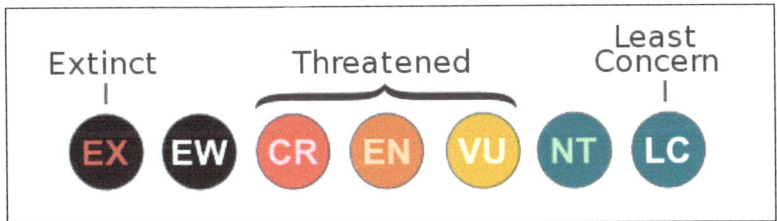

The list consists of 7 categories. From Least Concerned all the way to Extinct. Here are the definitions of each category:

- **LEAST CONCERN (LC):** A species that has been evaluated but not qualified for any other category on the list.
- **NEAR THREATENED (NT):** A species that may be considered threatened with extinction in the near future.
- **VULNERABLE (VU):** A species likely to become endangered unless the circumstances that are threatening its survival and reproduction improve.
- **ENDANGERED (EN):** A species that is considered very likely to become extinct.
- **CRITICALLY ENDANGERED (CR):** A species that is facing an extremely high risk of becoming extinct in the wild.
- **EXTINCT IN THE WILD (EW):** A species that is only known by living members kept in captivity or as a naturalized population outside its historic range due to massive habitat loss.
- **EXTINCT (EX):** A species that has been terminated.

Learn about the REPTILES

Before you start coloring, it's important to learn where the reptiles in this book live or lived and know their conservation status. Many of them are doing well and thriving and are considered least concern; a few are vulnerable or threatened while the dinosaurs are long extinct.

❱ Armadillo Girdled Lizard
They live in desert areas along the western coast of South Africa. It takes its tail in its mouth and rolls into a ball when frightened.
Conservation Status: Least Concern

❱ Attenborough's Fan-Throated Lizard
Discovered in 2016, it is found in coastal Kerala in southern India and named after Sir David Attenborough an English broadcaster and natural historian.
Conservation Status: Unknown

❱ Bush Viper
Found only in tropical subsaharan Africa and can grow to 31 inches long.
Conservation Status: Some species are Threatened

❱ Green Sea Turtle
It lives throughout tropical and subtropical seas around the world. It is a protected species in most countries.
Conservation Status: Endangered

❱ Iguana
Native to tropical areas of Mexico, Central America, South America, and the Caribbean.
Conservation Status: Least Concern

❱ Komodo Dragon
Lives on the Indonesian islands of Komodo, Rinca, Flores, and Gili Motang. It is the largest extant species of lizard.
Conservation Status: Vunerable

❱ Lesser Chameleon
Endemic to Madagascar. It is threatened by habitat loss as a result of quartz and tourmaline mining.
Conservation Status: Endangered

❱ Mosasaurus
Lived from about 82 to 66 million years ago and had a maximum length of up to 17.6 meters (58 feet)
Status: Extinct

❱ Mountain Horned Dragon
Found in the tropical forests of Cambodia and southern Vietnam.
Conservation Status: Least Concern

❱ Parasaurolophus
Lived during the Late Cretaceous Period, about 76.5–73 million years ago in what is now North America and possibly Asia.
Status: Extinct

❱ Pinocchio Lizard
Its currently known habitat is a small stretch of vegetation along an Ecuadorian highway. It was thought to be extinct until its rediscovery in 2004.
Conservation Status: Endangered

❱ Stegosaurus
Lived during the Late Jurassic period 155 and 150 million years ago in the western United States and Portugal.
Status: Extinct

❱ Thorny Devil
Endemic to Australia, It grows up to 21 cm (8.3 in) in total length (including tail).
Conservation Status: Least Concern

❱ Triceratops
Lived in the late Cretaceous period, about 68 million years ago in mya in what is now North America
Status: Extinct

❱ Tyrannosaurus Rex
Lived throughout what is now western North America, on what was then an island continent known as Laramidia during the Cretaceous period, 68 to 66 million years ago.
Status: Extinct

REPTILES Index

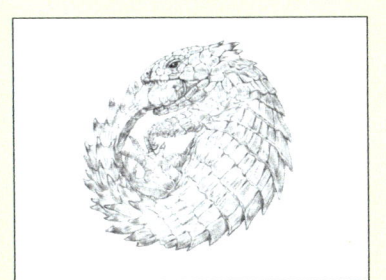
Armadillo Girdled Lizard 1

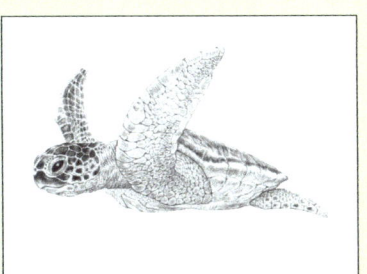
Green Sea Turtle 4

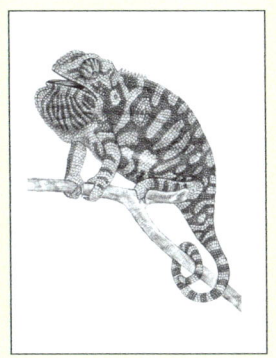
Lesser Chameleon 7

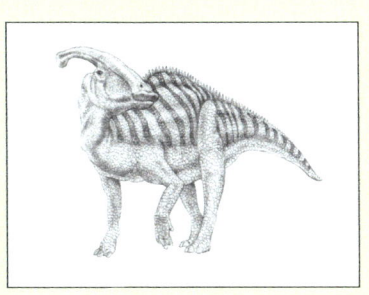
Parasaurolophus 10

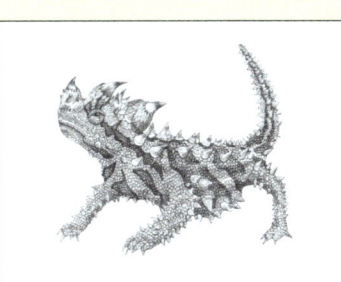
Thorny Devil 13

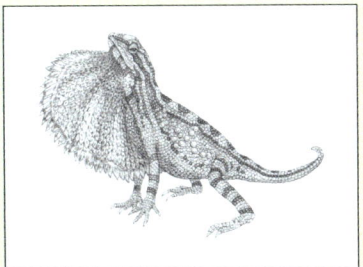
Attenborough's Fan-Throated Lizard 2

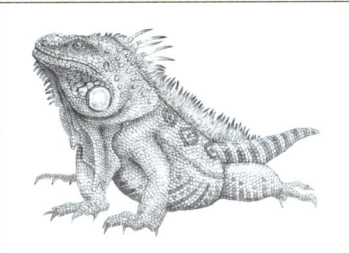
Iguana 5

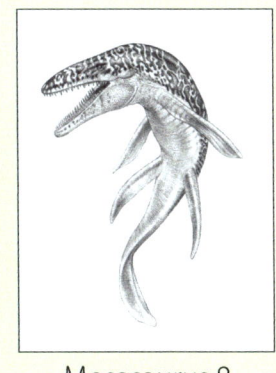
Mosasaurus 8

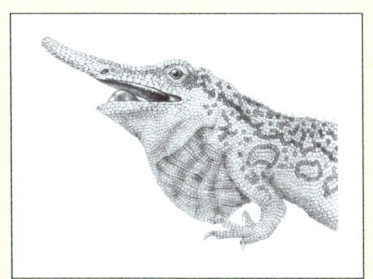
Pinocchio Lizard 11

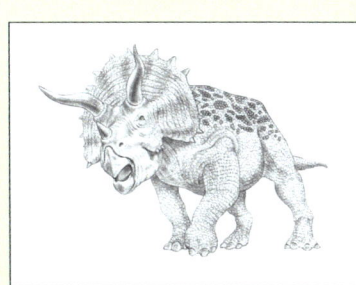
Triceratops 14

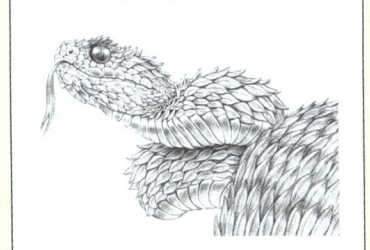
Bush Viper 3

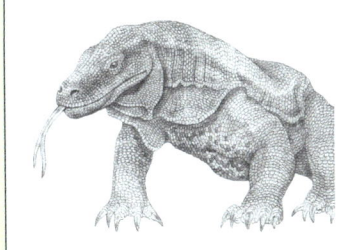
Komodo Dragon 6

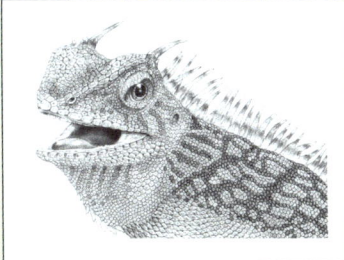
Mountain Horned Dragon 9

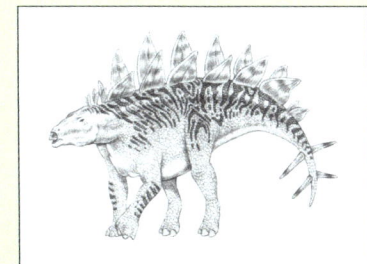
Stegosaurus 12

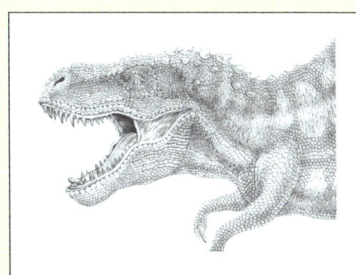
Tyrannosaurus Rex 15

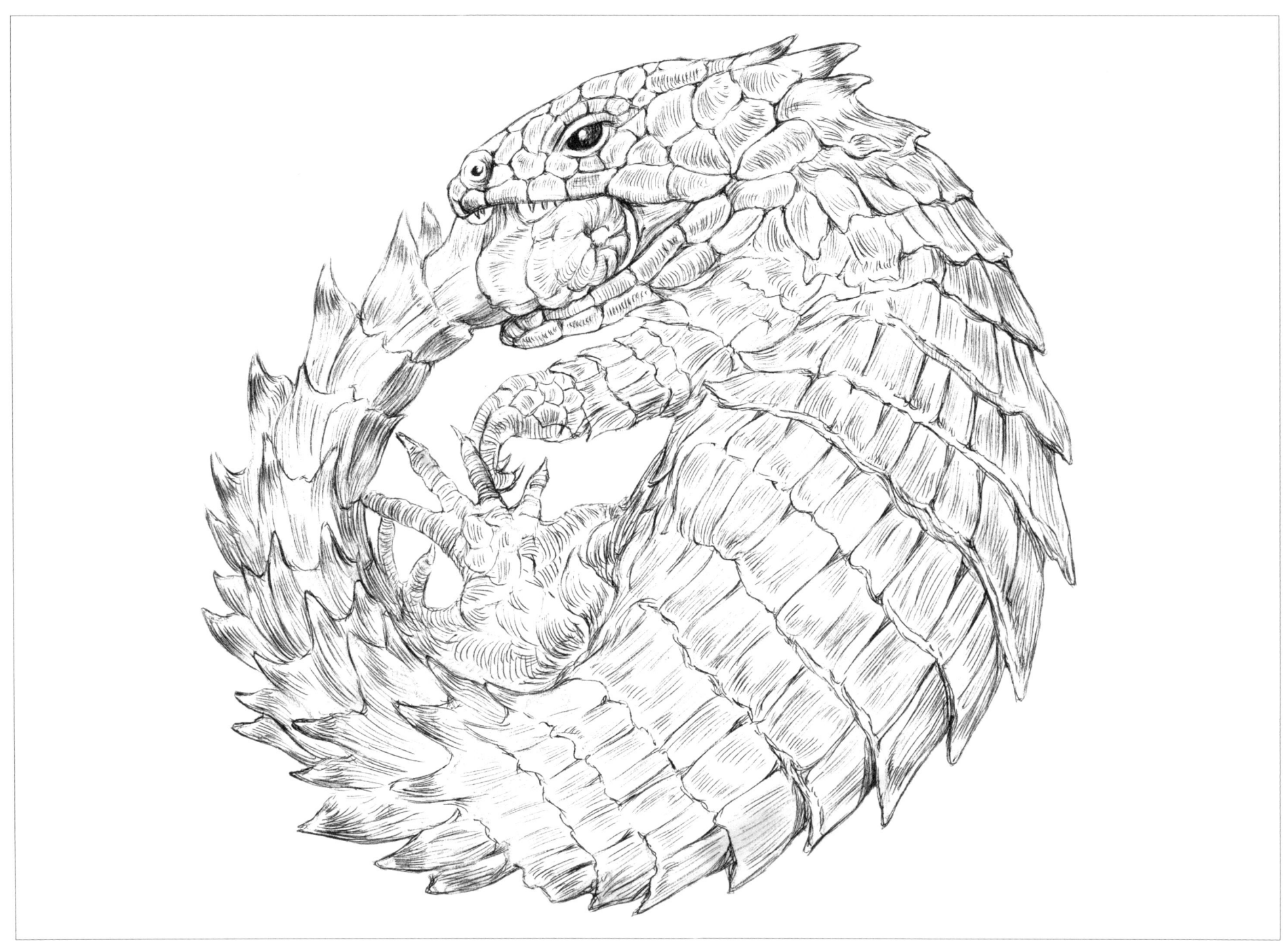

Armadillo Girdled Lizard

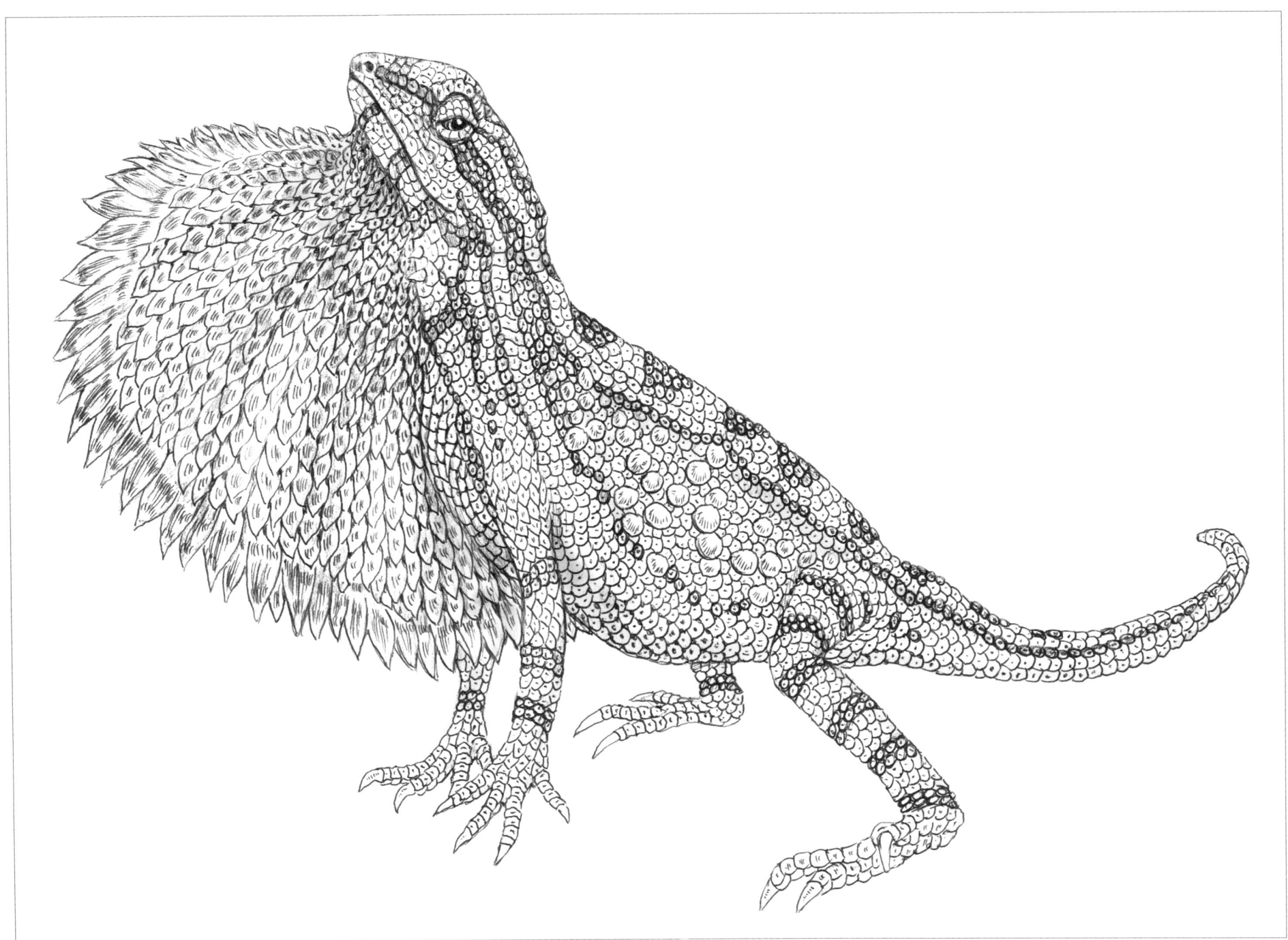

Attenborough's Fan-Throated Lizard

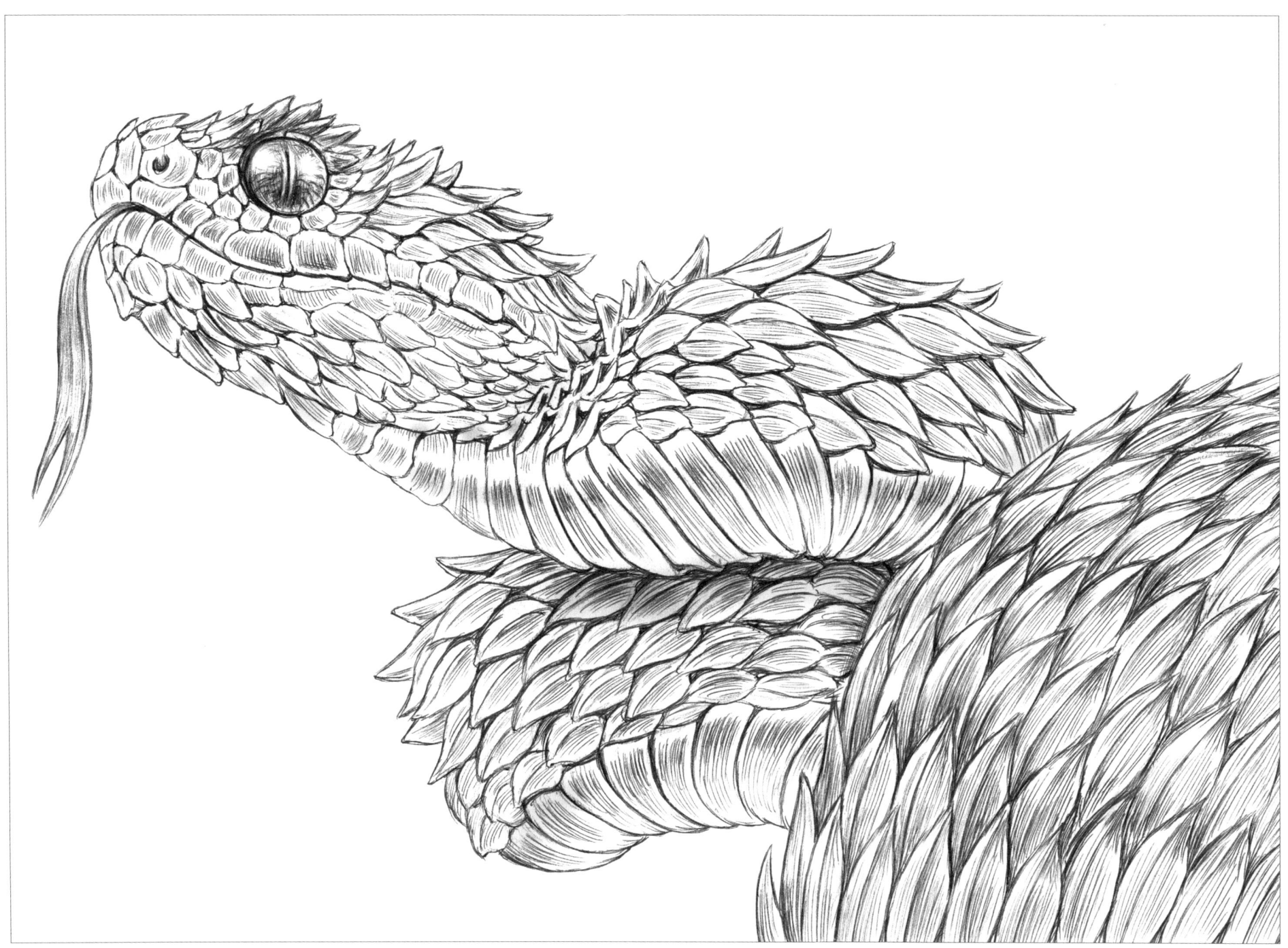

Bush Viper

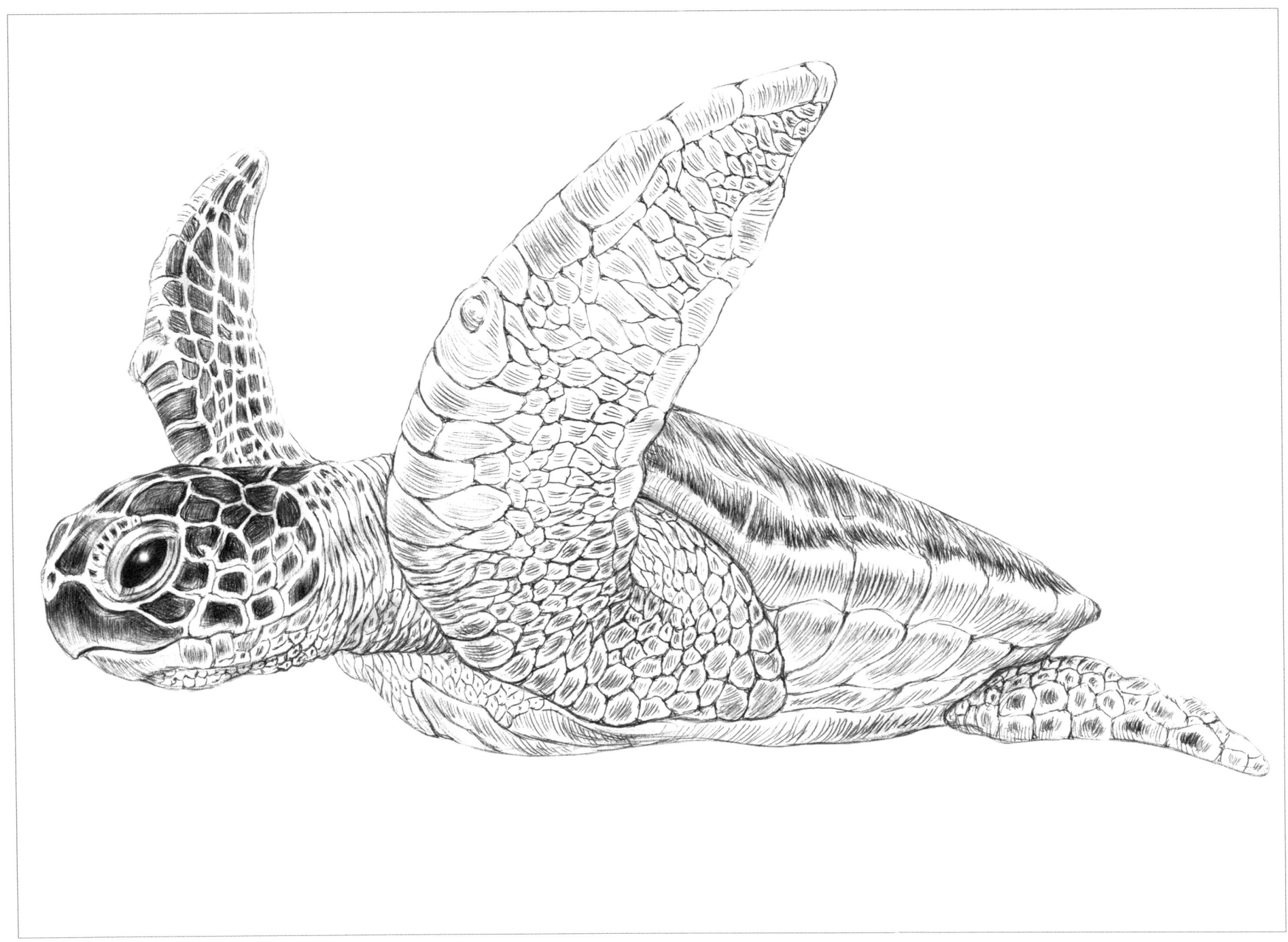

Green Sea Turtle

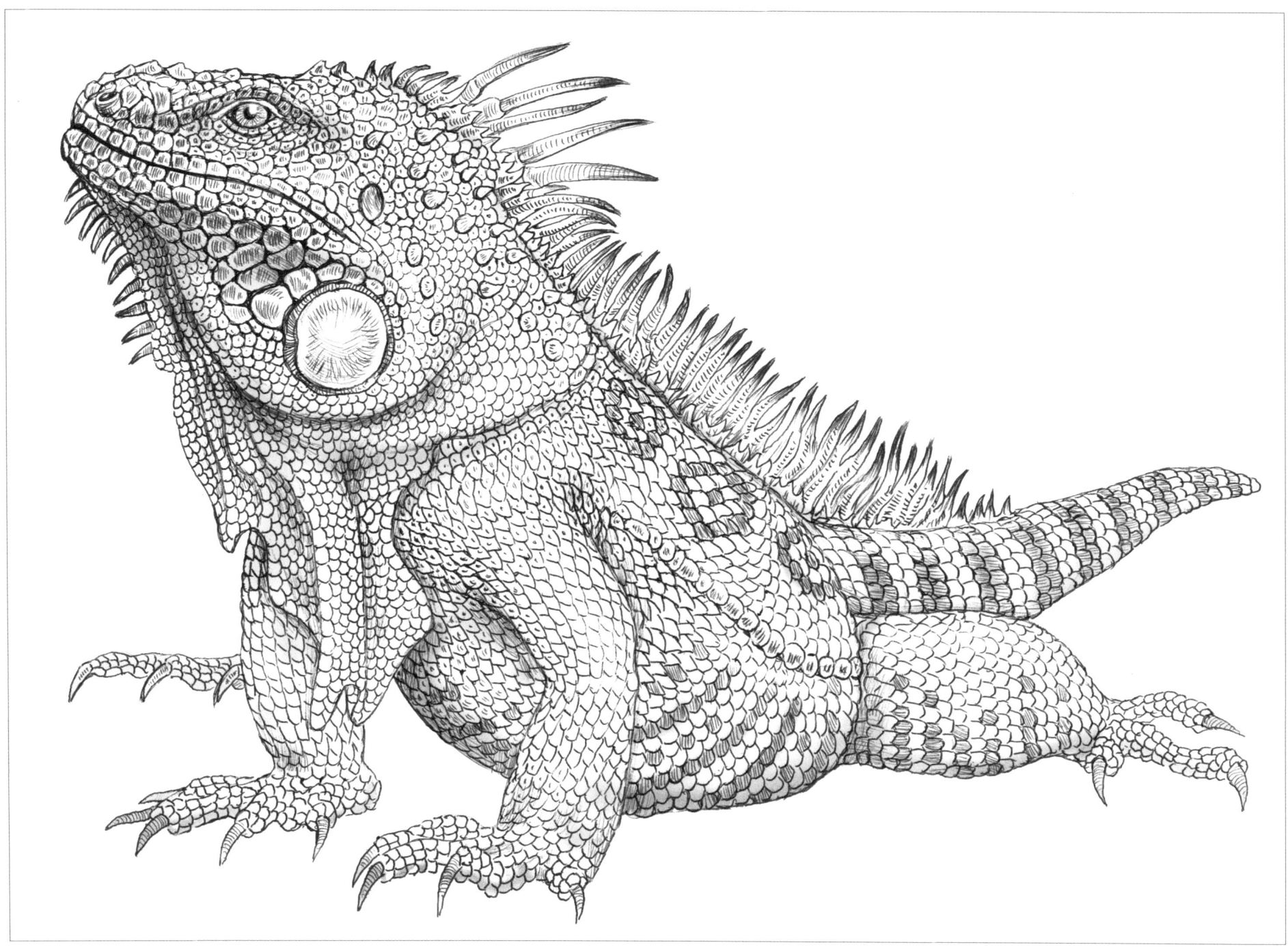

Iguana

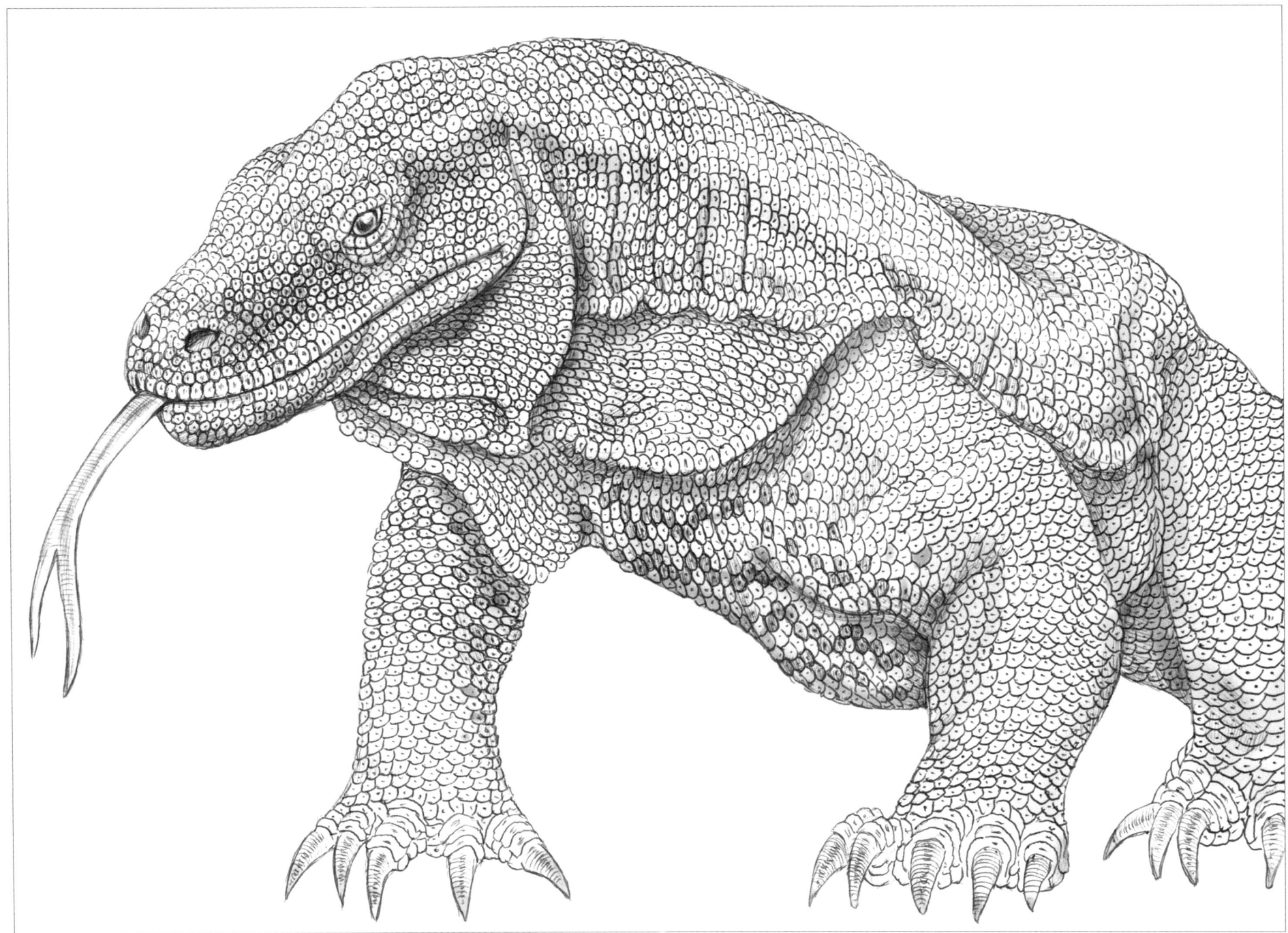

Komodo Dragon

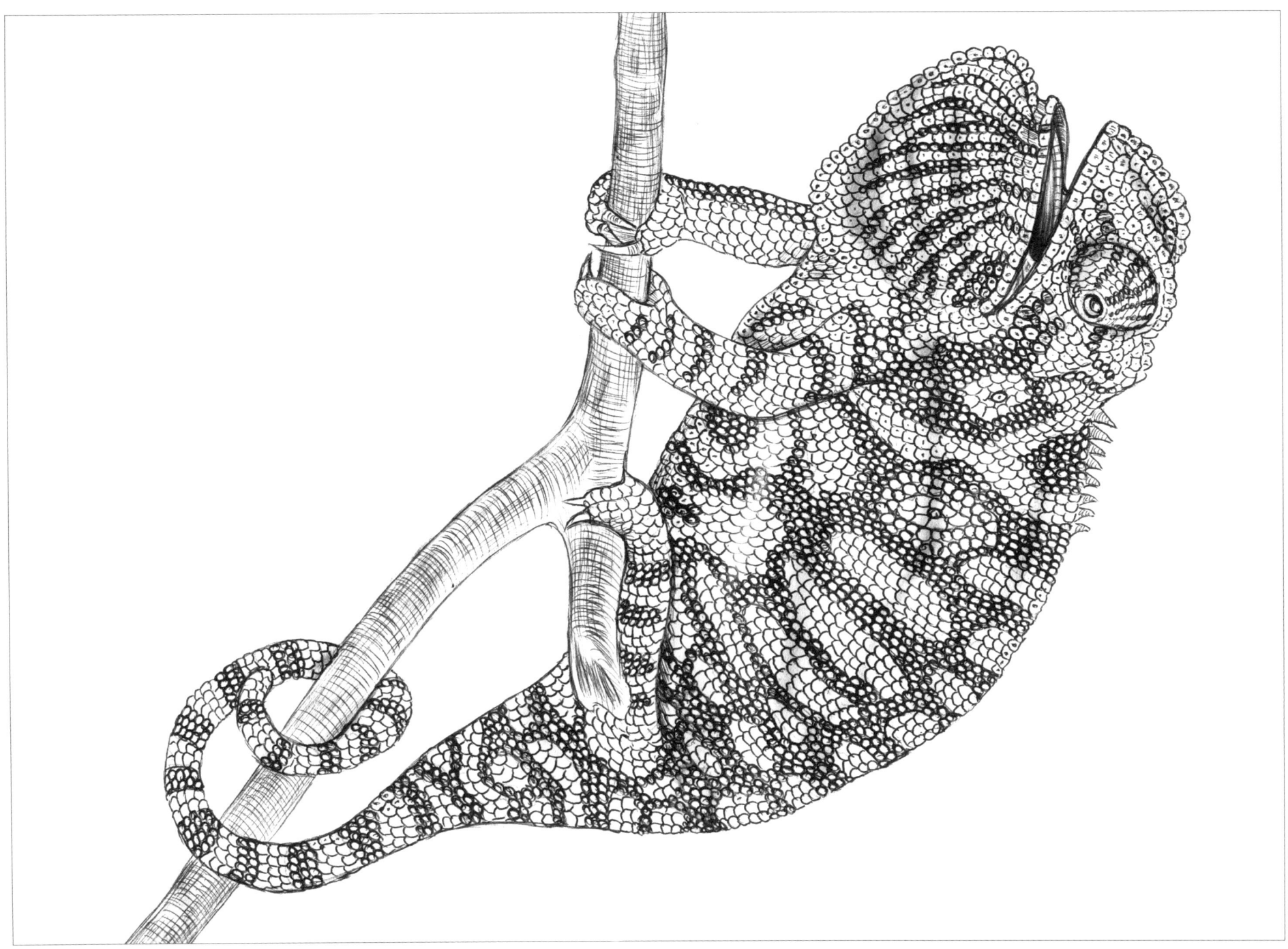

Lesser Chameleon

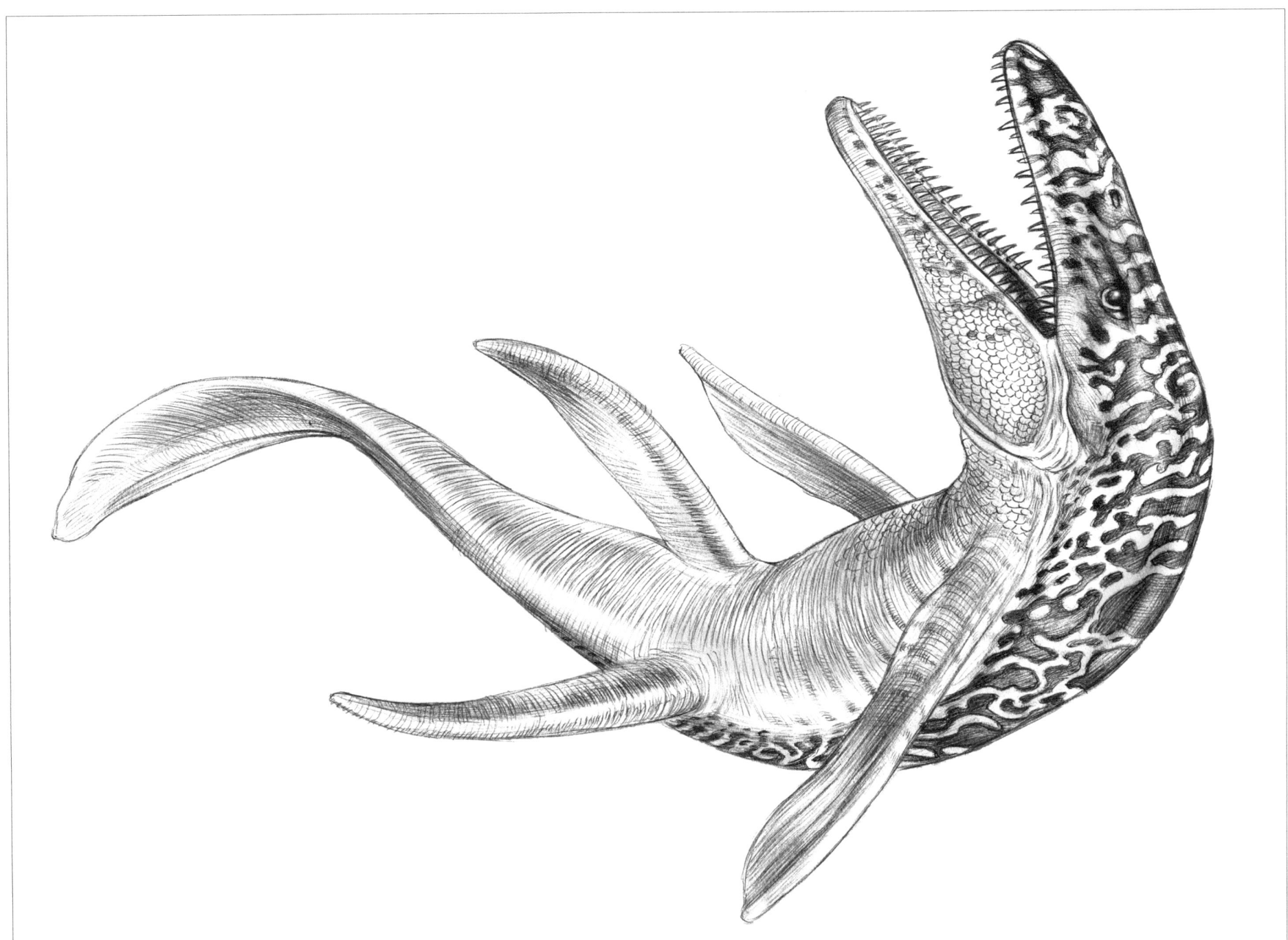

Mosasaurus

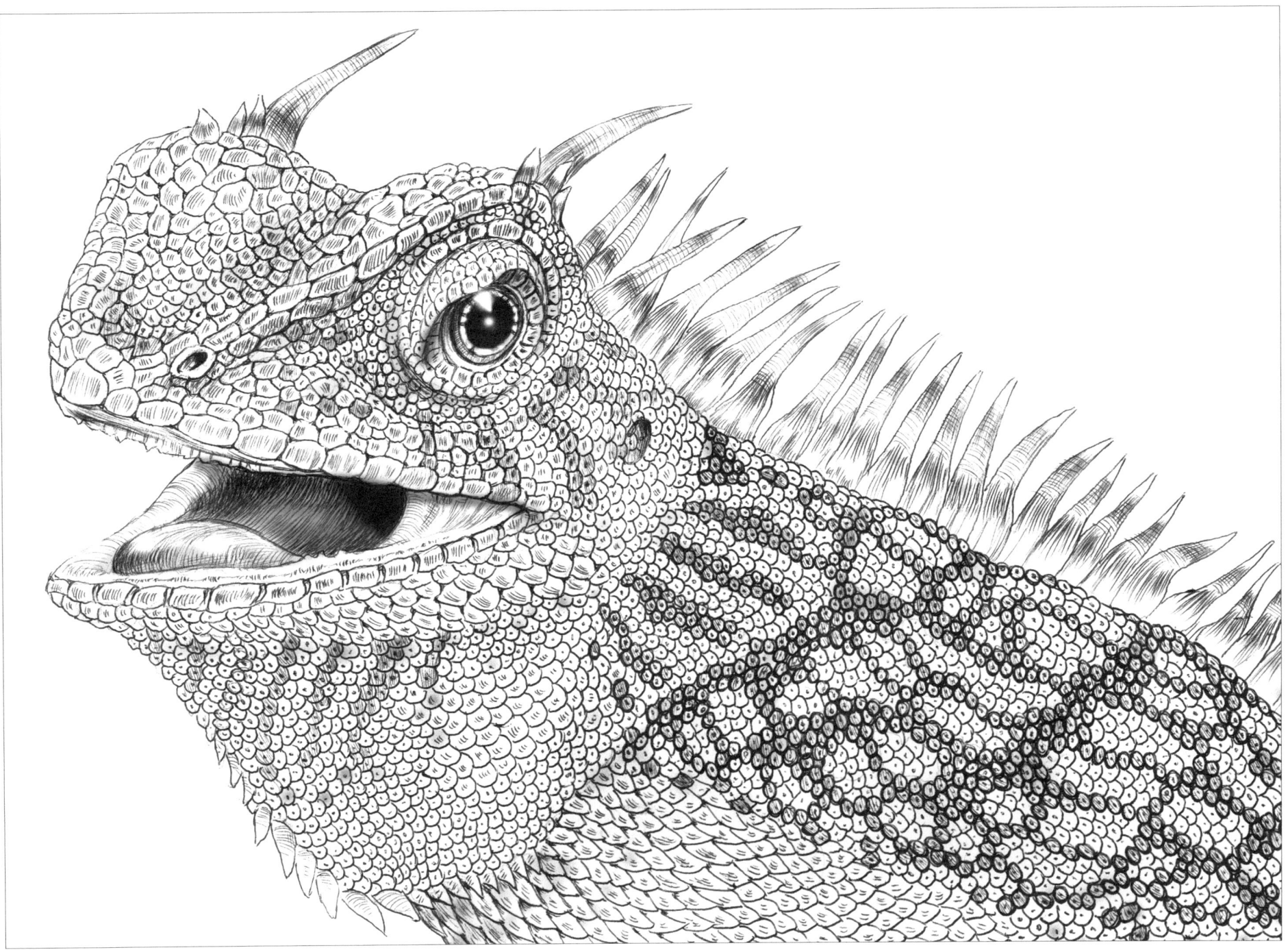
Mountain Horned Dragon

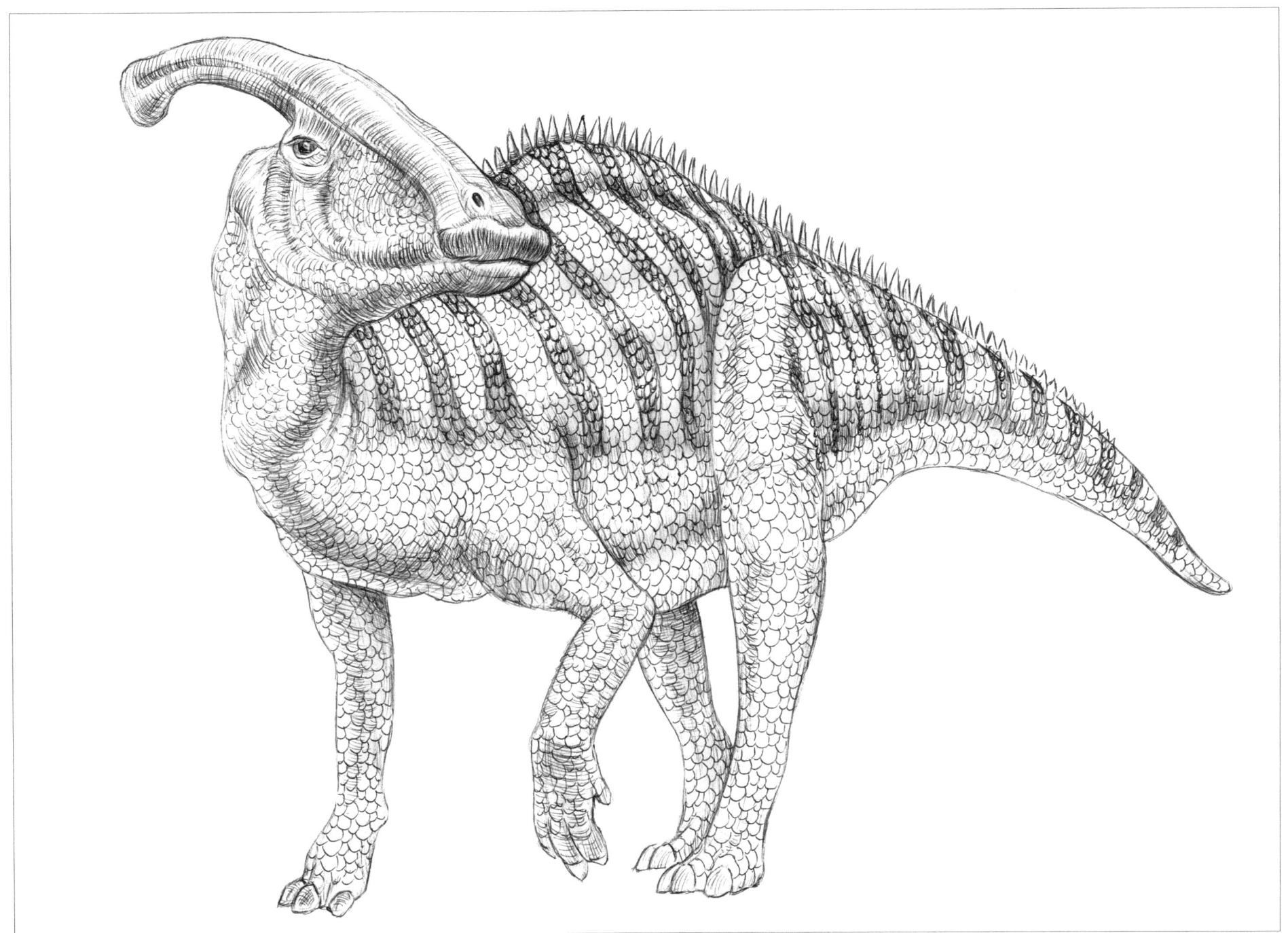

Parasaurolophus

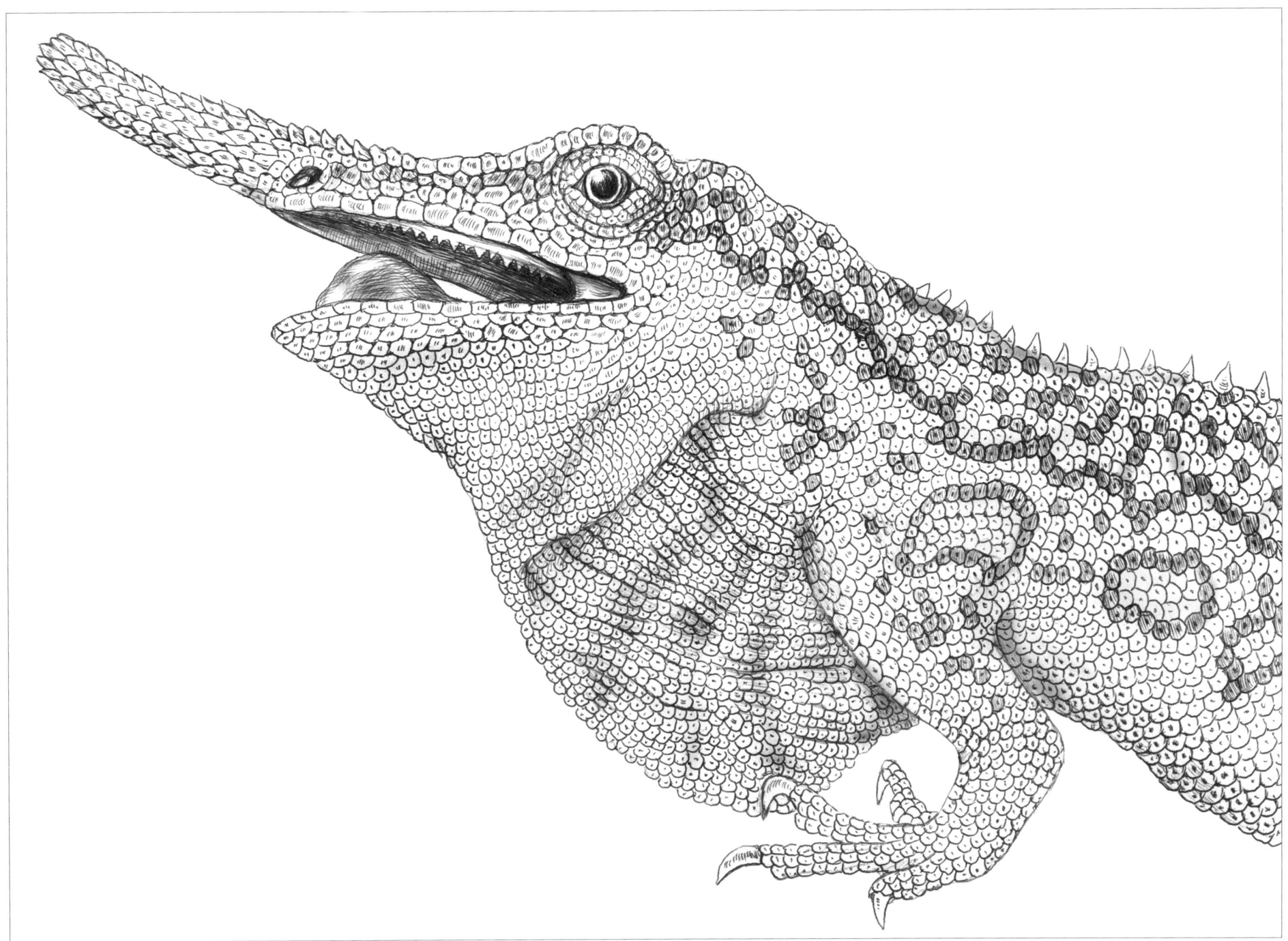

Pinocchio Lizard

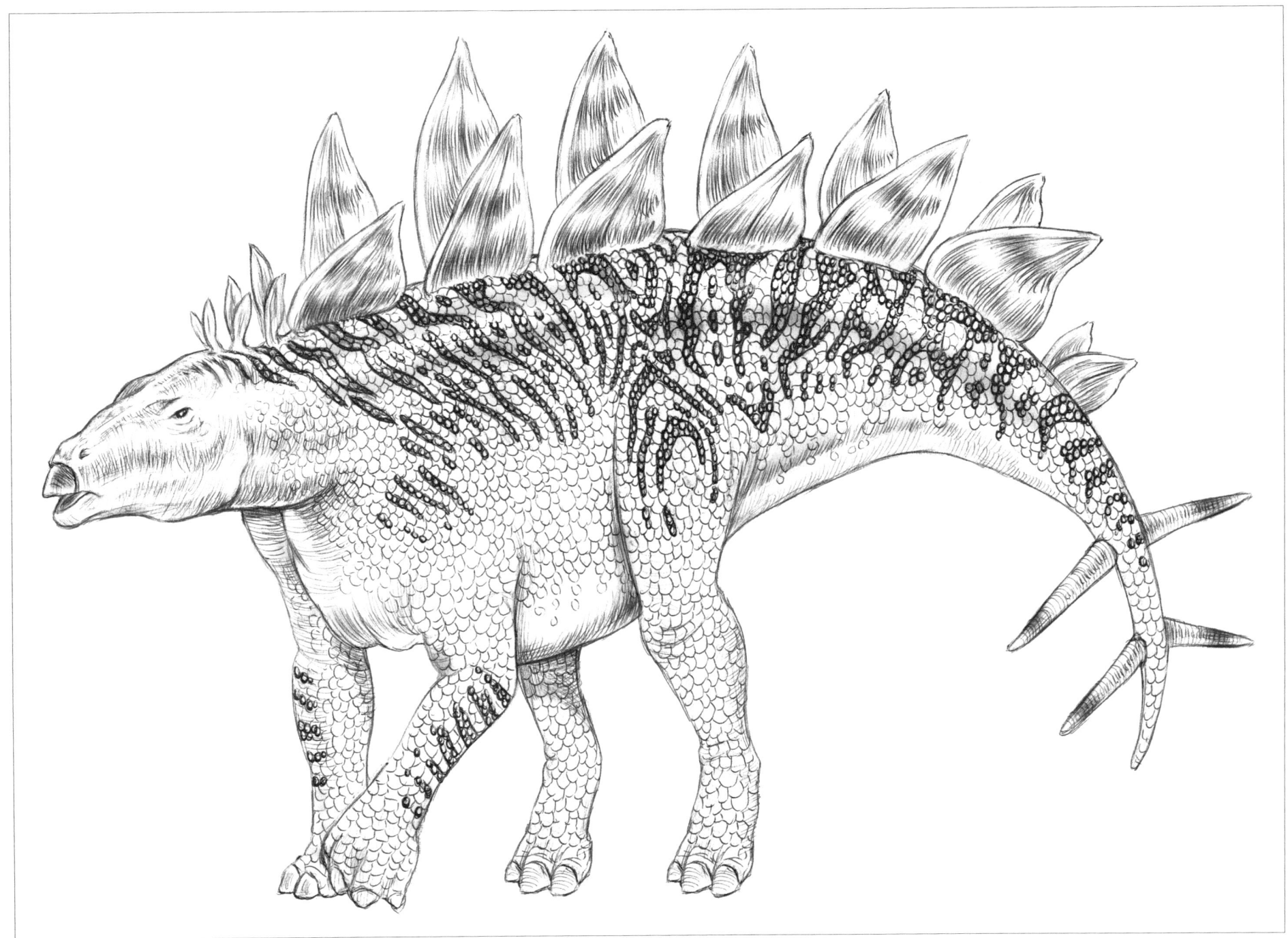

Stegosaurus

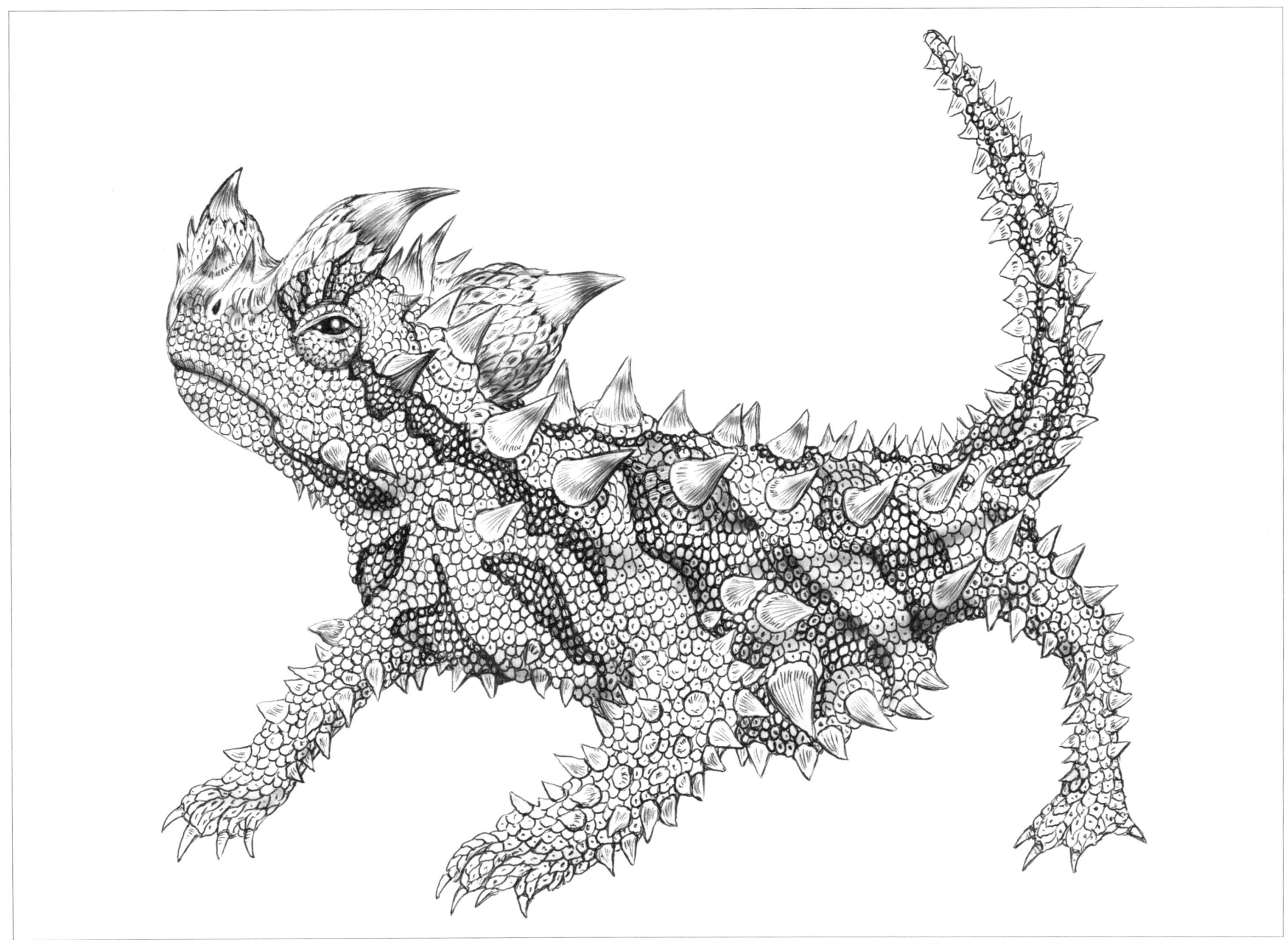

Thorny Devil

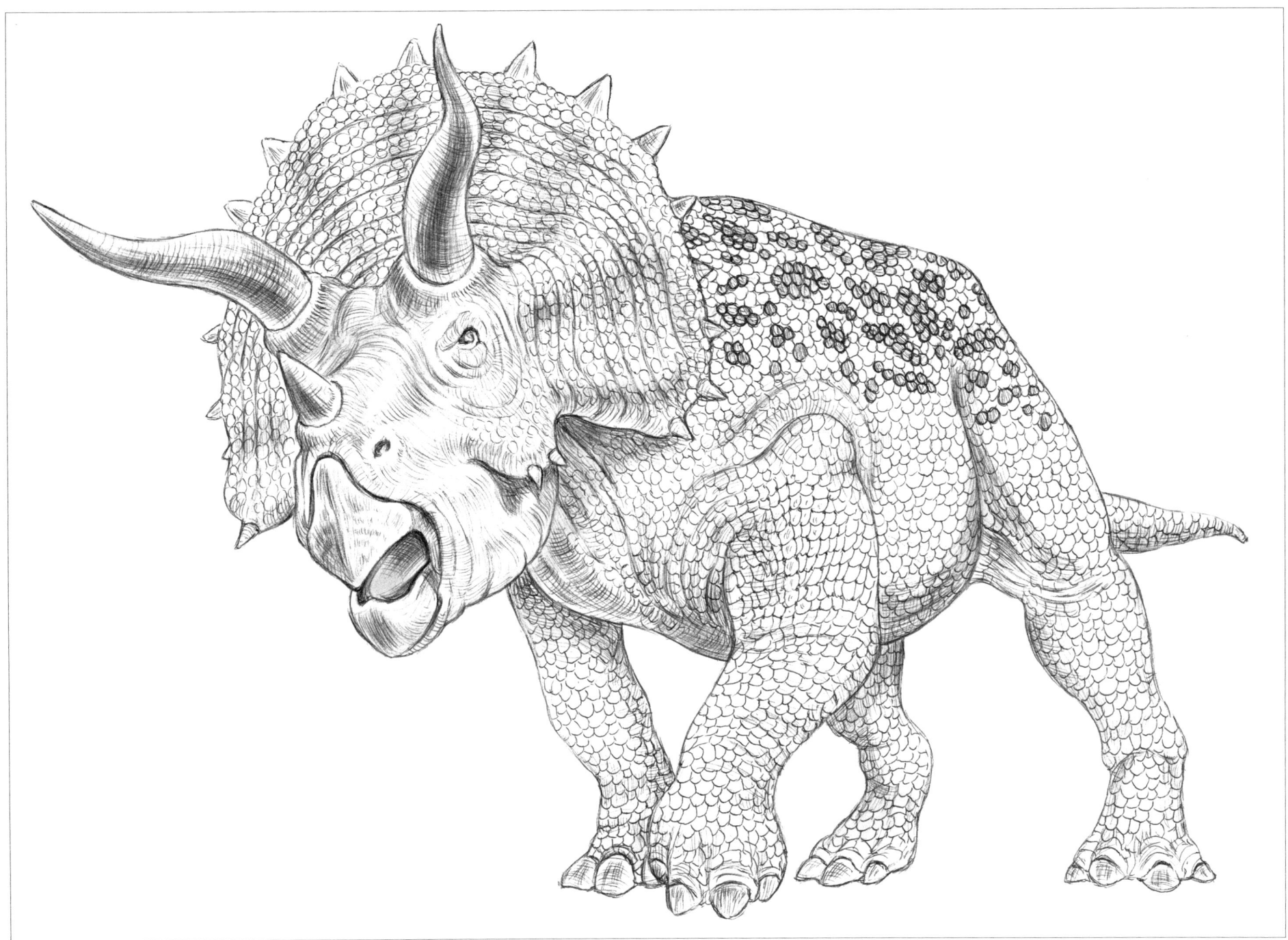

Triceratops

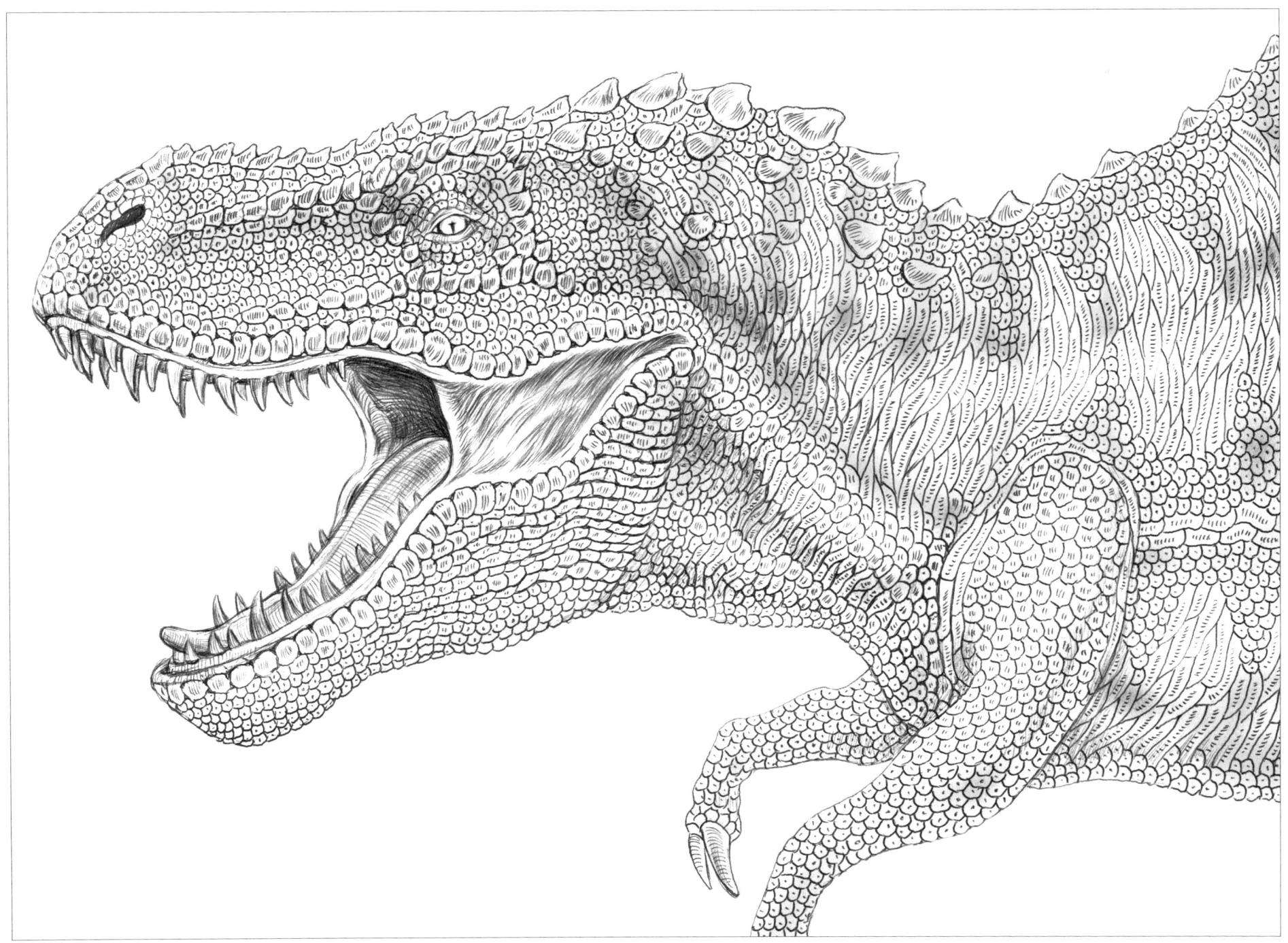

Tyrannosaurus Rex

Tim Jeffs is a New York City based artist and illustrator who has been creating dynamic artwork for over 25 years. Animals are a favorite subject matter of his, along with the complex and intricate details these creatures possess. "*The incredible diversity and complexity of animals has always intrigued me. They offer endless pleasure to look and marvel upon. In every drawing I try to capture the unique quality of each particular animal. I hope you enjoy my perspective, love and admiration of these incredible creatures.*"

Visit my website for prints, digital coloring books and coloring lessons:

www.TimJeffsArt.com

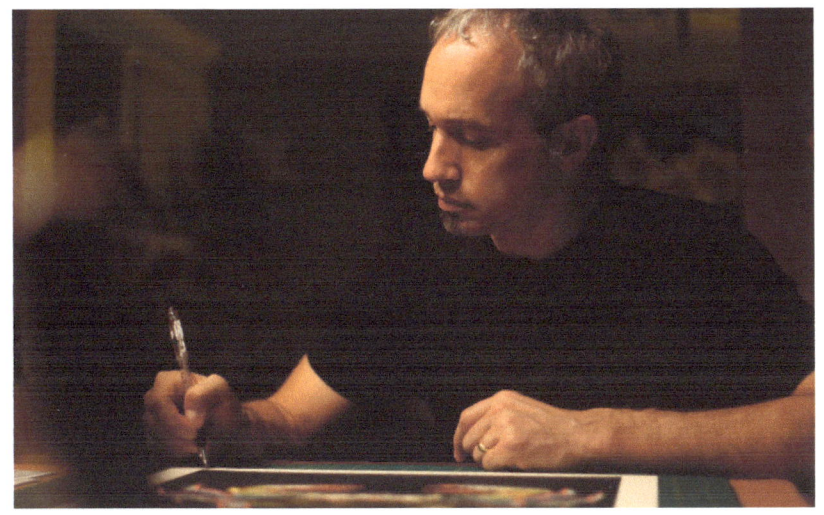

Discover the full line of Tim Jeffs' Published Coloring Books

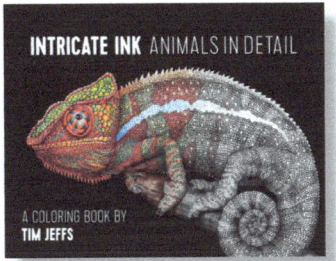
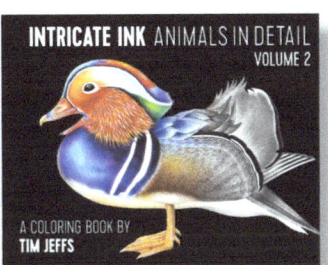
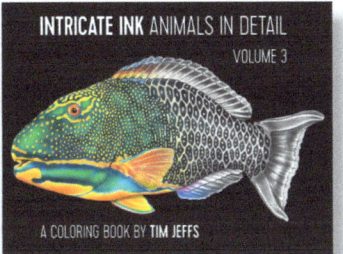
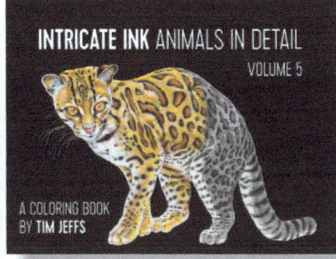
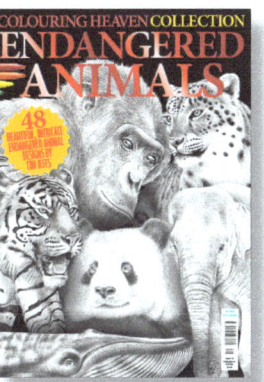

Intricate Ink Animals In Detail Volume 1, 2 3 and 5 Available at:
Pomegranate.com
Amazon.com
Bookdepository.com

**Colouring Heaven Collection
Endangered Animals**
Available at: Colouringheaven.com

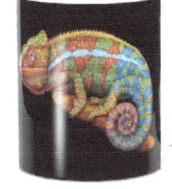

Discover Tim Jeffs' Merchandise

Etsy Shop
www.etsy.com/shop/TimJeffsArt

Society6 Shop
www.society6.com/TimJeffsArt

Redbubble Shop
TimJeffsArt.redbubble.com

Vsual Print Shop
https://vsual.co/shop/tim-jeffs-art

Discover the full line of Tim Jeffs Digital Coloring Books at:
www.TimJeffsArt.com

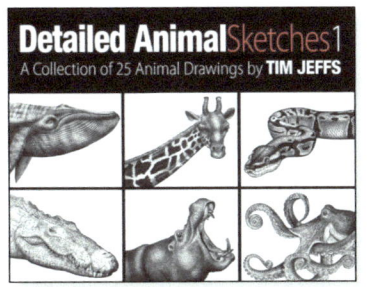
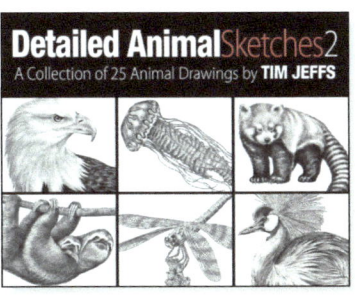
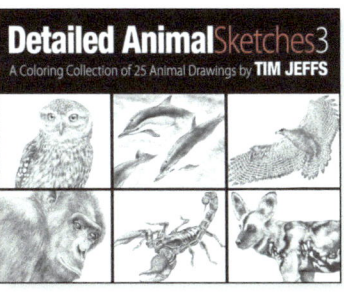
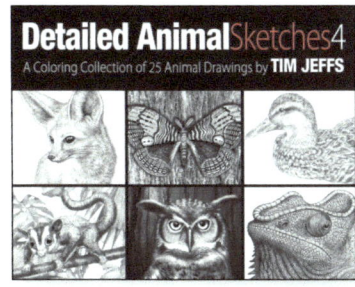
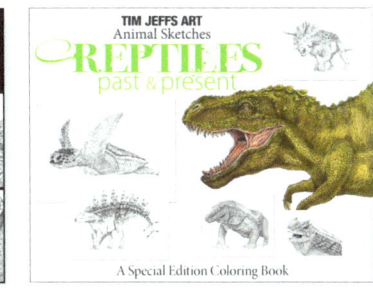
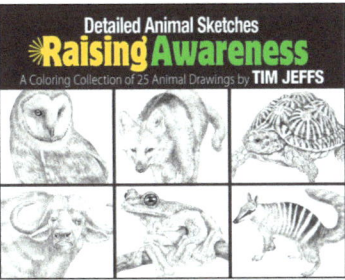
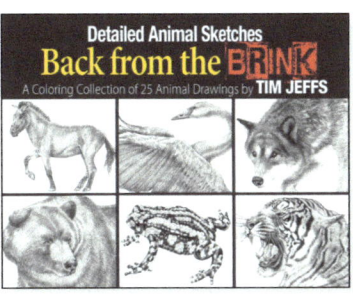
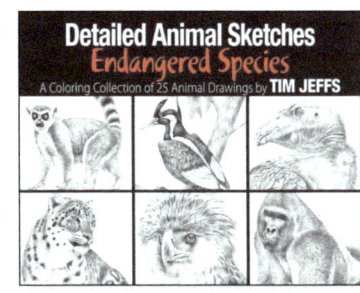
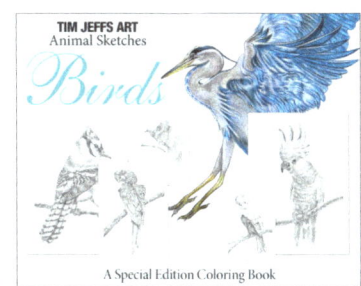
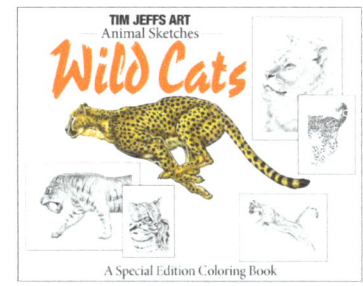

And Coloring Lessons

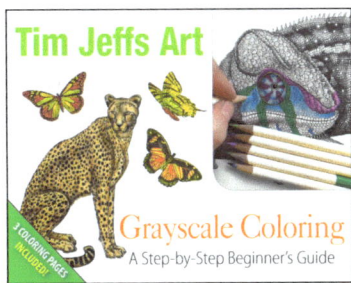
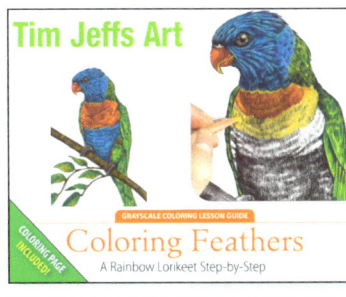
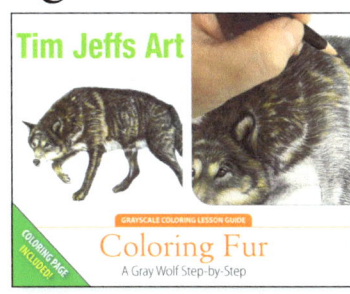
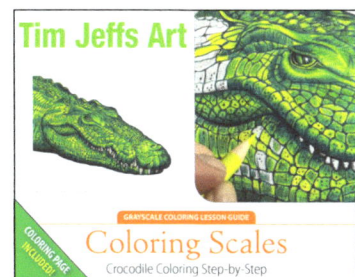
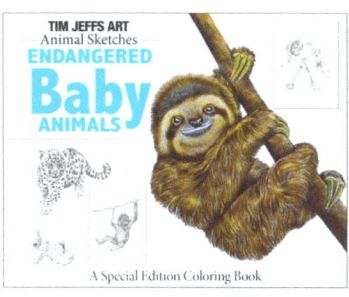
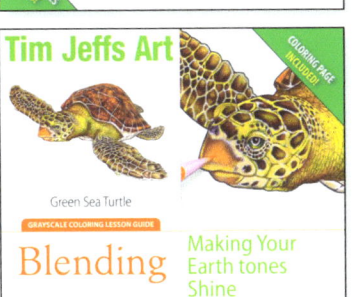
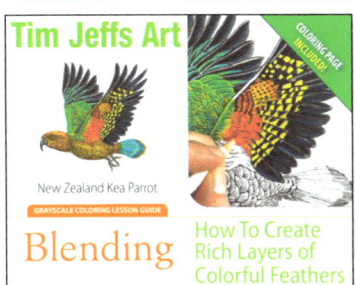
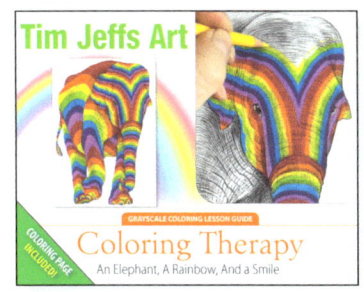
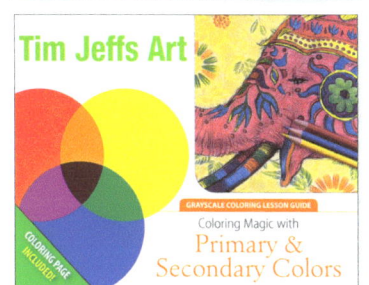
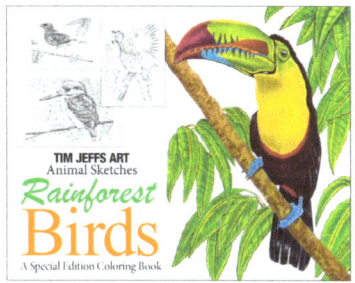

TIM JEFFS ART Online Resources

Share Your Creativity with the World!

Join the ever-expanding coloring group of animal lovers who inspire each other through their colorings of the animals from Tim's books and lessons. With thousands of members from all around the world, Tim's Facebook group "Intricate Ink Coloring Group" is a creative and safe space where everyone is welcome. Jo Warren, the groups all-inspiring administrator will welcome you in with open arms and is there to encourage everyone to just have fun no matter your coloring skill level. Come join, we can't wait to have you as a member! Join Tim's Facebook Coloring Group at:

www.facebook.com/groups/intricateink

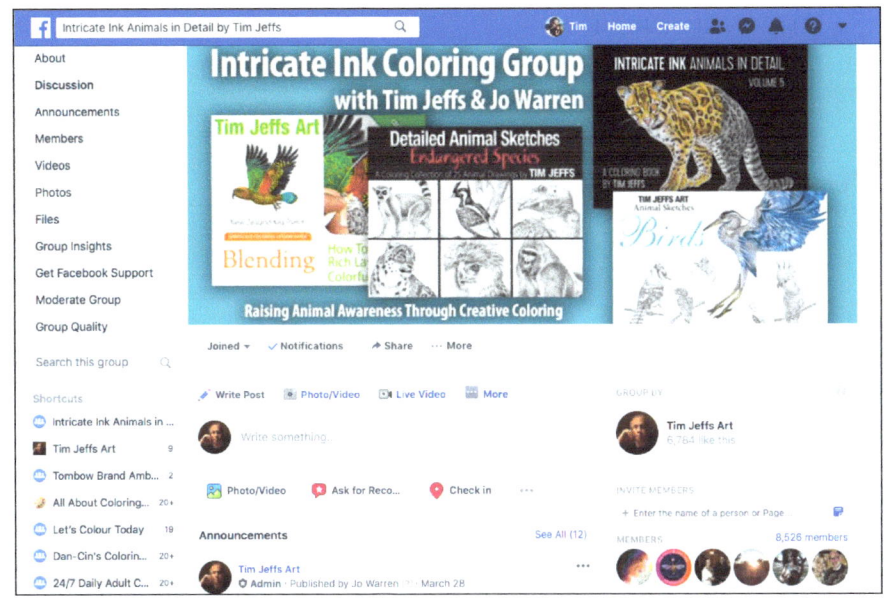

Visit the Home of Tim Jeffs Art

TimJeffsArt.com is my home on the web where I display all of my work and various projects. I hope you can stop by for a visit! You'll find my new shop where signed and unsigned prints of all of my animal drawings are available to purchase, along with the complete library of my digital download coloring books and grayscale coloring lessons. In the conservation section, you can see the projects that I am very proud of. Using my art to preserve wildlife is so important to me.

www.TimJeffsArt.com

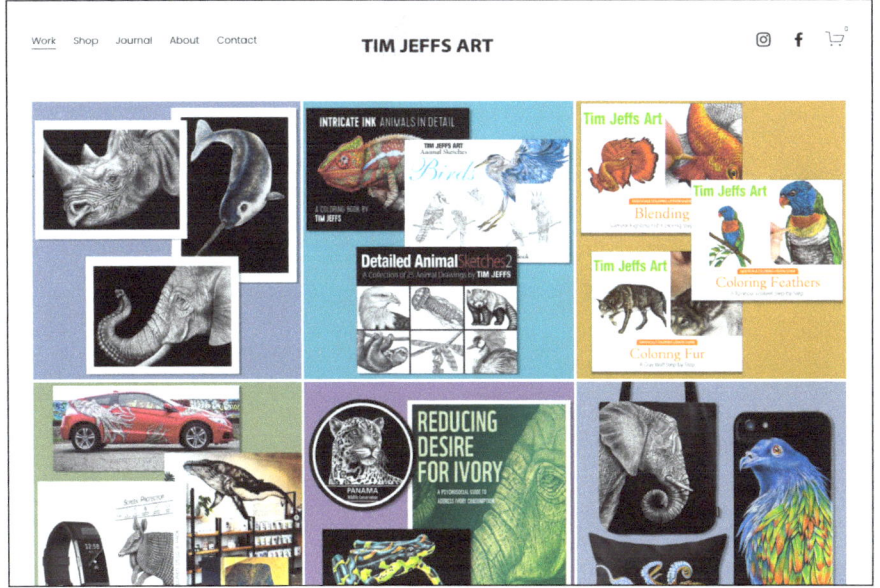

www.ingramcontent.com/pod-product-compliance
Lightning Source LLC
Chambersburg PA
CBHW051221220526
45473CB00003B/1125

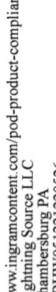